CHICKENS AND GOATS
Copyright © 2011 by Mnyandu Publishing

mnyandupublishing@gmail.com

ISBN 978-0-9869764-1-4

for our father

"ROBOT"

Mongezi Mnyende
20 August 2011

a robot man that tells you to go or to stop.

"A STRONG MAN ON STAGE"

Monireza Muzafari
20 Aug 2021

the strong man has come to fight the army that is threatening to kill him.

he told the people that he will fight the army.

he is going to win because he won the first champion of his life, before.

he can kill people in a push of a button, and they fall on the floor.

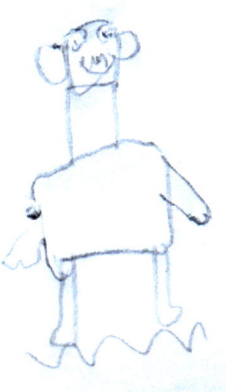

"ROBOT"   Mangezi Muganda   20 Aug 2011

the robot sits on the grass, it's dead.

no one is going to bury it, they are just going to put a new battery and it will come back to life.

"ME AND MY SHEEP"

Mongezi
Mnyandu
20 Aug 2011

I am feeding it the food and I am going to slaughter it and make isiphandla.

I know we make it with a goat not a sheep. sheep doesn't cry but the goat does.

"GOAT ON THE STREET, CLOUD HANGING OVER"

got

Monrez Muyonde 20 Aug 2011

the goat is going nowhere but to the farm because there is no grass on the street.

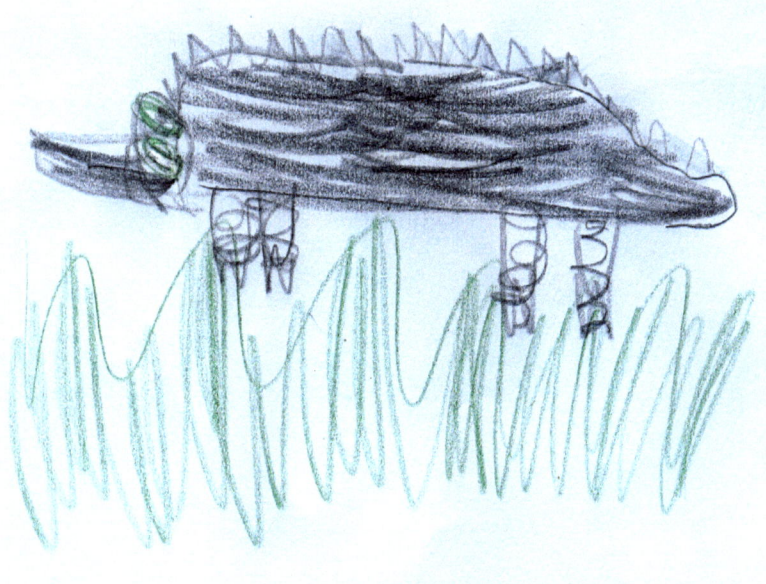

"SPOTTING CROCODILE"

Mongezi Mkunyandu 20 Aug 2011

looking for a person to swallow.

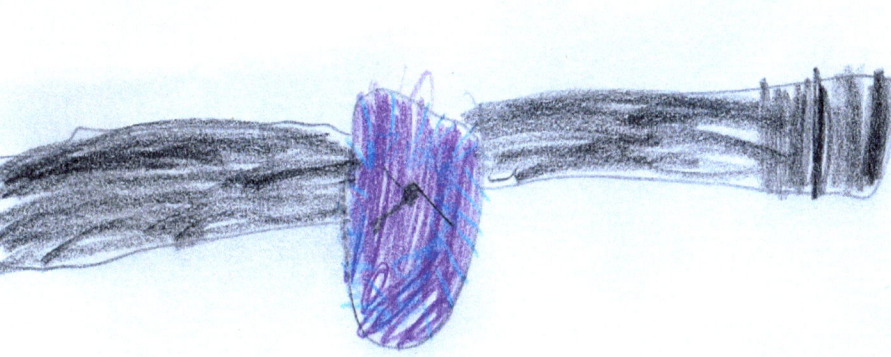

Mengezi Munyandu 20 Aug 2011

my watch is good.

it is half past three.

my daddy must wear the watch.

he must put batteries under.

"SPECIAL BUTTERFLY"

Mangezi Mnguandu 20 Aug 20..

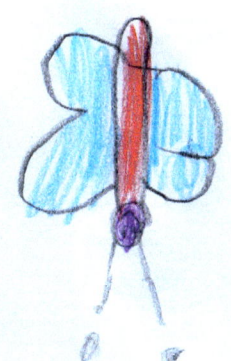

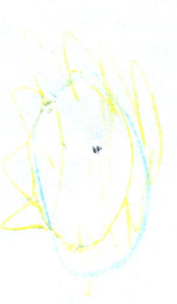

it can fly to heaven but it is dead already.

people made it, and they put a rope on it.

My tit

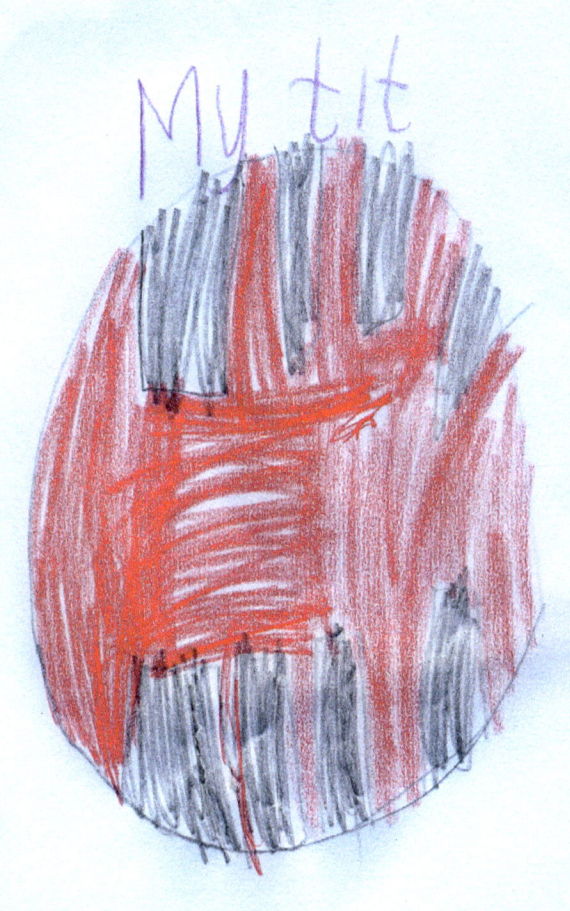

"MY TEETH"

Monpezi Myandu
20 August 2011

I never wash them so they are rotten.

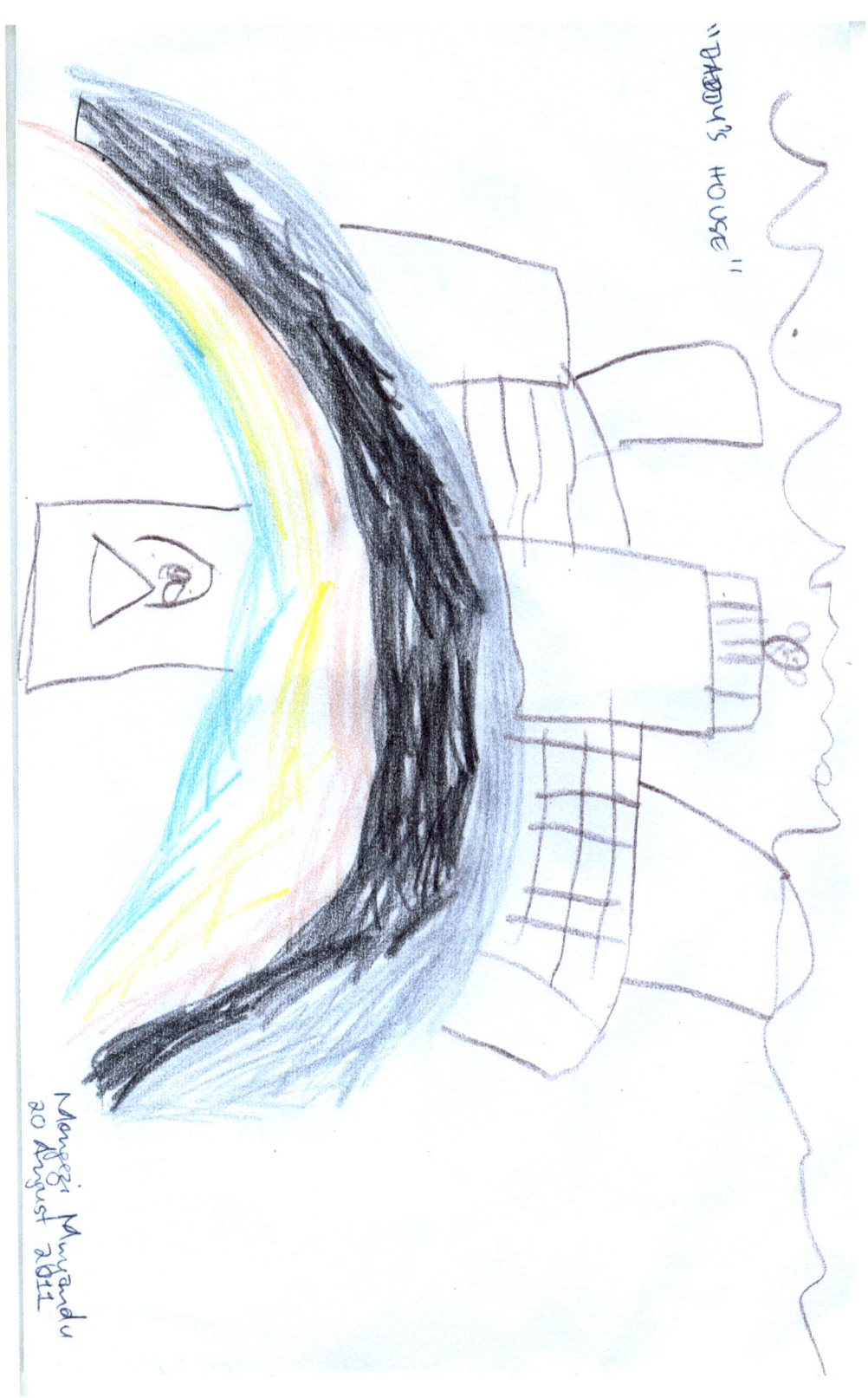

"DADDY's HOUSE"

Manyasi Muyandu
20 August 2011

my father lives in it and his younger brother is his next door neighbour.

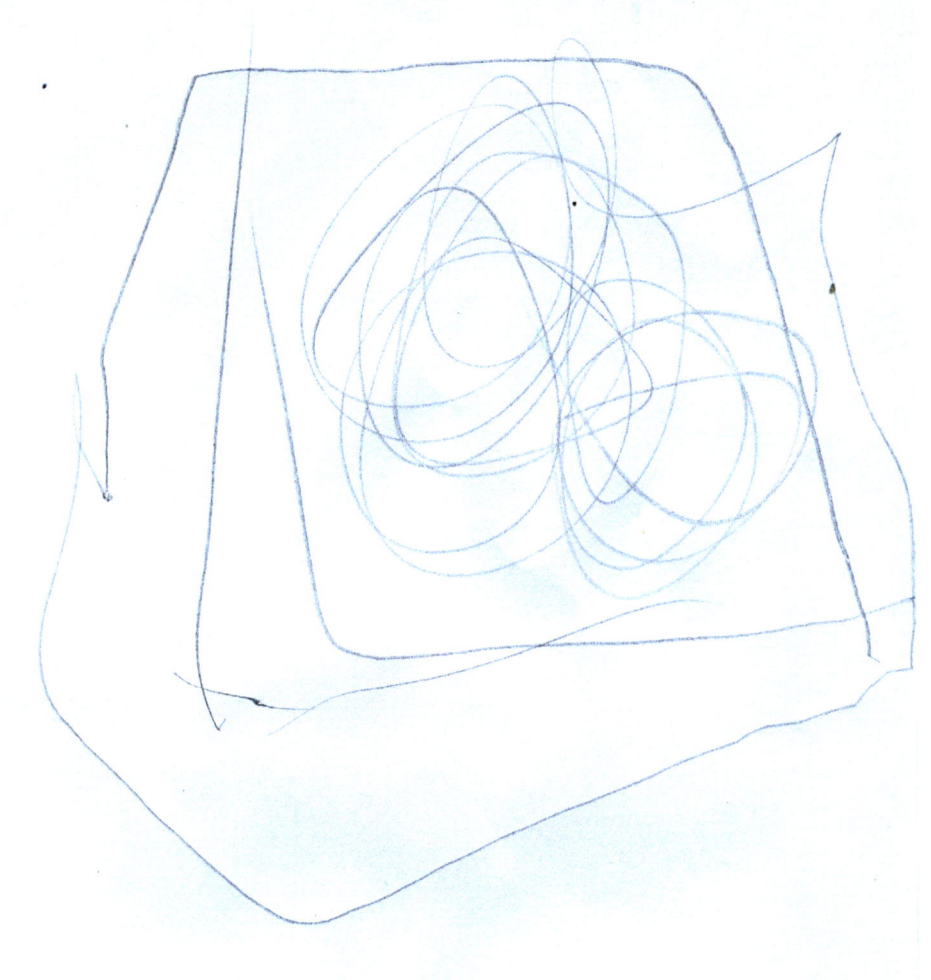

" COUCH "

Nandi
Miranda
20 Aug 2011

a small couch.

my friends will sit on it.

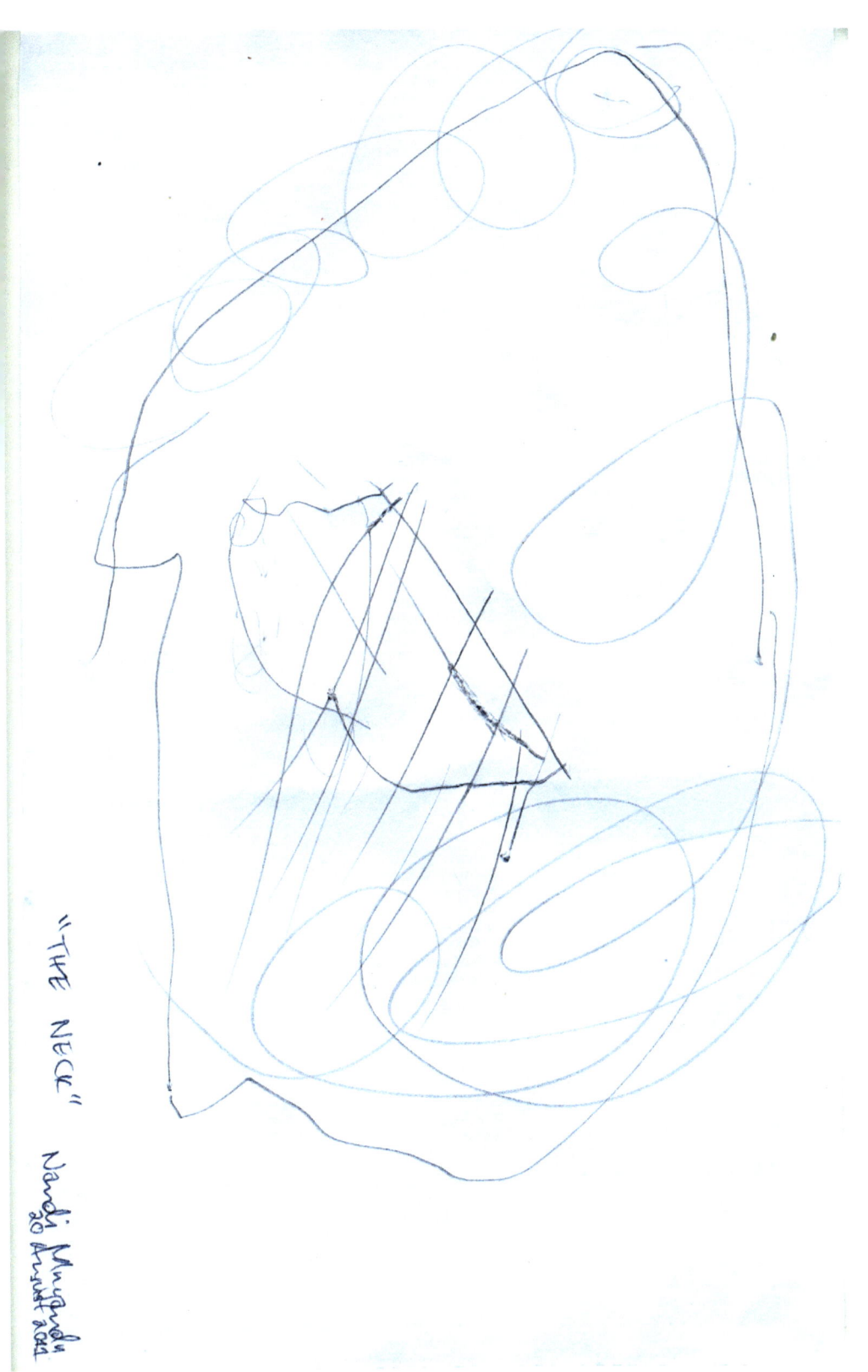

"THE NECK"

Nandi Mngondi
30 August 2021

my (her) neck.

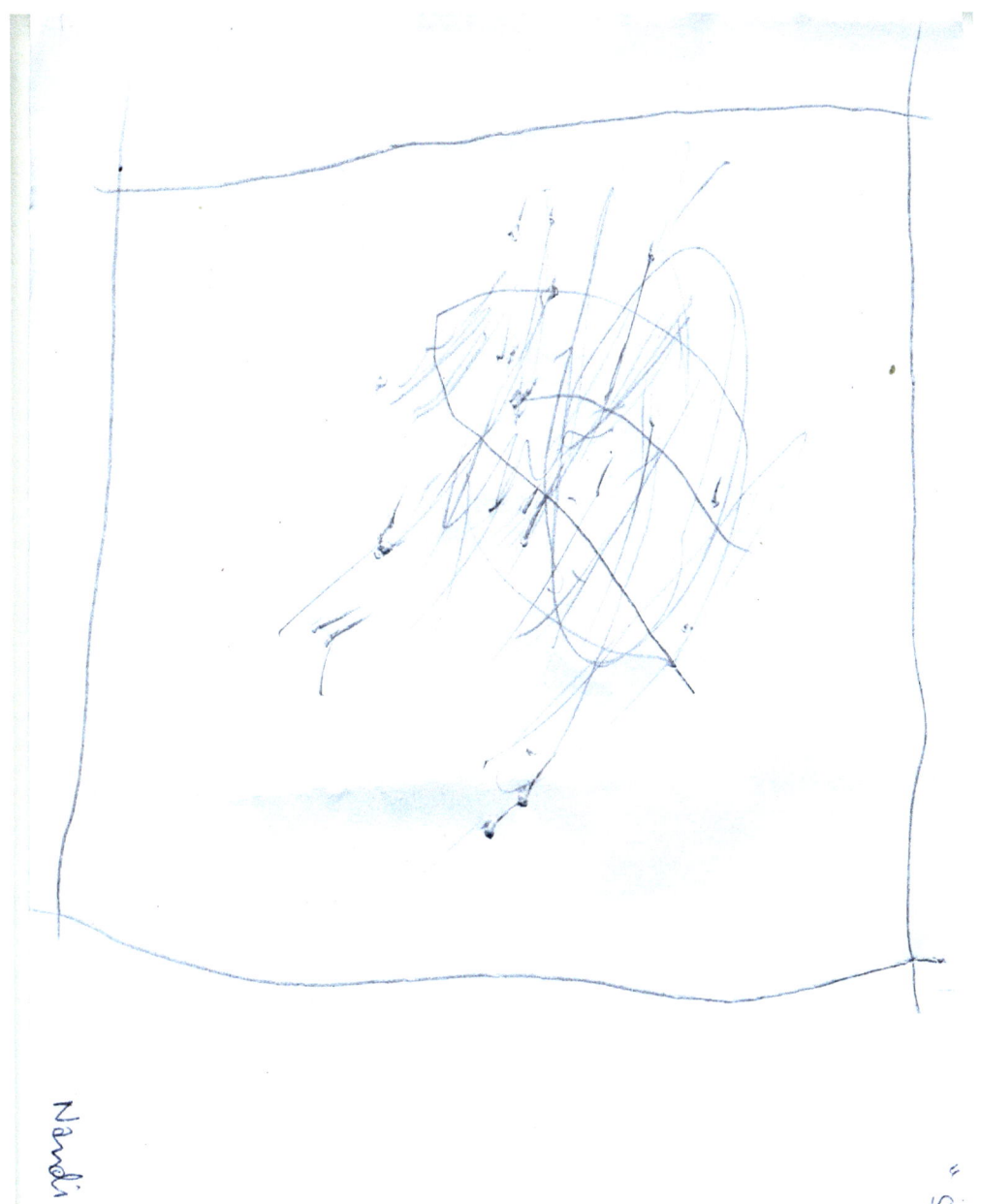

Nandi Muyard 20 August 2011

" SQUARE HOUSE "

for daddy, mommy and my brother.

my brother is planting food outside.

daddy is inside, sitting.

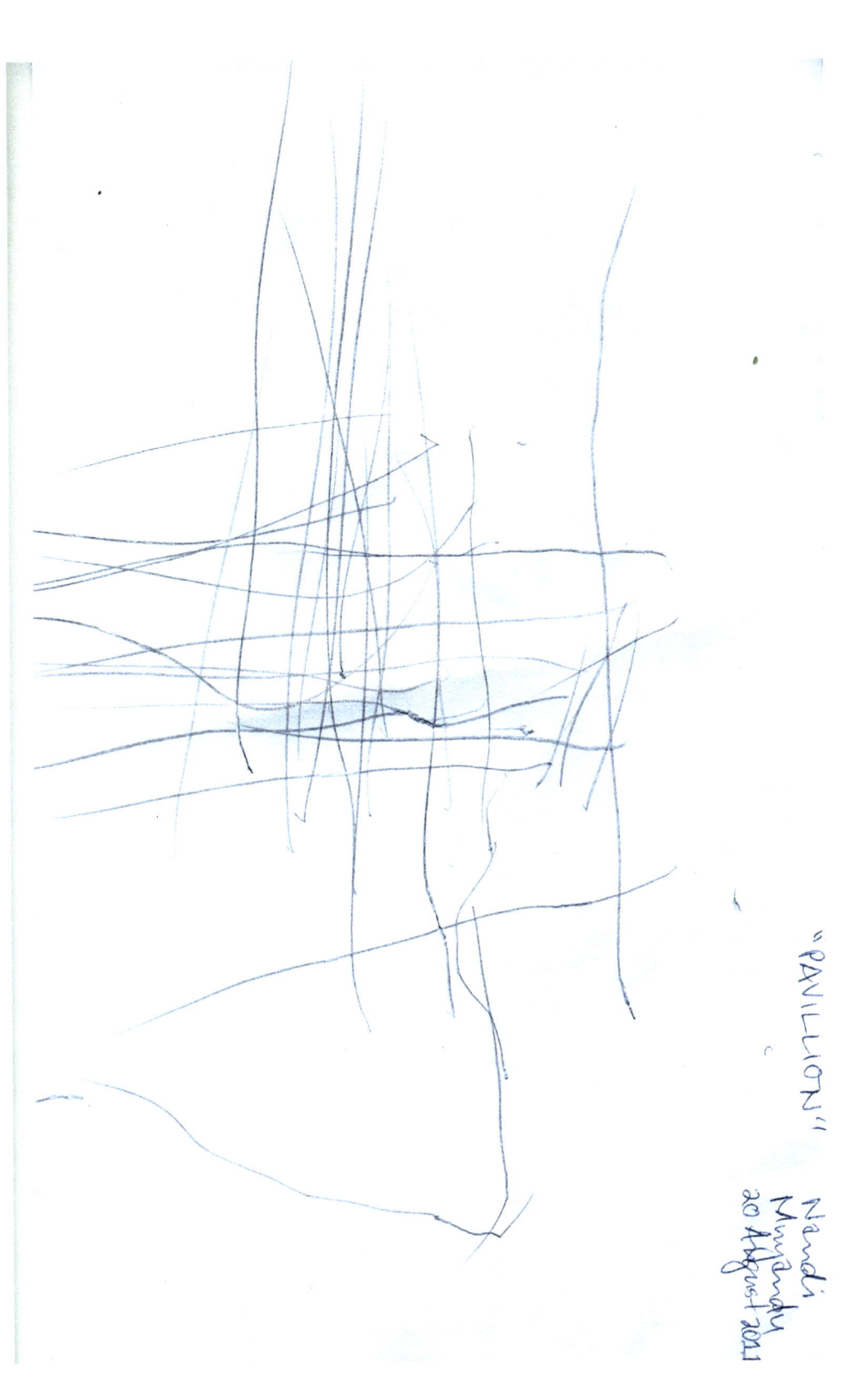

"PAVILLION"

Nandi
Miranda
20 August 2021

to buy kitty shoes.

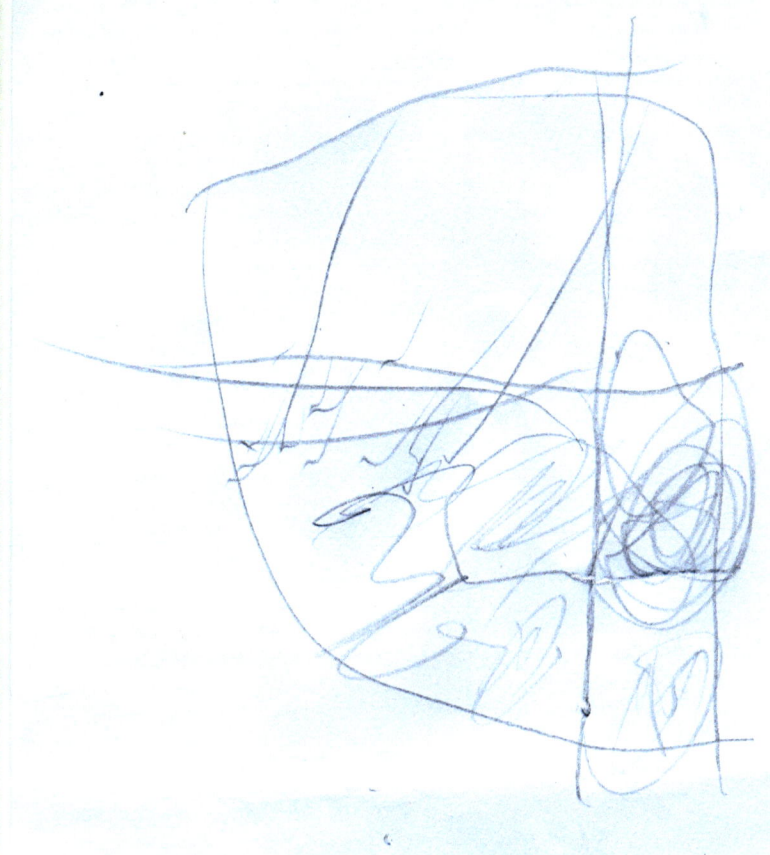

"N"

Nandi Nkambai
20 Aug 2012

sharpening the pen so I can draw a rainbow.

"BRAIN"

Nandi Murphy
20 Aug 2011

"THE ATLAS"

Nandi Mhlanga
20 August 2012

" NICE BEAUTIFUL SQUARE RAINBOW "

Nandi Murambi
20 August 2019

20 August 2014

Nandi
Minyanda

"RAINBOW"

Nandi Muyanda
20 Aug 2014